COPYRIGHT NOTICE

Copyright © 2019 by Diego Rodriguez

All rights reserved for personal use only to purchaser of this material. All material is copyrighted for exclusive use by Diego Rodriguez as consulting and educational materials. No parts of this document in any way may be reproduced in any form. Anyone other than the purchaser who is not authorized to use, photocopy, sell or distribute this material will be prosecuted to the full extent of the law.

All of our materials are protected under federal and state copyright laws. You may not make copies of any of the books, video or audio CD's, audio files, e-books, except for your own personal use. All materials you buy are licensed (or, in the case of other author's works, sublicensed) to End Users and not sold, not withstanding use of the terms "sell," "purchase," "order," or "buy" on the site. Your license is nonexclusive, nontransferable, non-sub licensable, limited and for use only for you, the end user, and you ONLY. That means you cannot sell, trade, copy, and assign, lease or license your rights of these materials.

TABLE OF CONTENTS

TABLE OF CONTENTS 3

LEGAL DISCLAIMER 4

DEDICATION 5

INTRODUCTION 7

Stream 1: Earned Income 11

Stream 2: Residual Income 13

Stream 3: Royalty Income 15

Stream 4: Interest Income 19

Stream 5: Dividend Income 25

Stream 6: Profit Income 33

Stream 7: Rental Income 39

Stream 8: Capital Gains 43

CONCLUSION 45

RESOURCES 47

Copyright © 2019 by Diego Rodriguez

LEGAL DISCLAIMER

The publisher and author make no representations or warranties with respect to the accuracy or completeness of the contents of this work and specifically disclaim all warranties, including, without limitation, warranties of fitness for a particular purpose. No warranty may be created or suitable for every situation. This work is sold with the understanding that the publisher and author are not engaged in rendering legal, accounting, or other professional services. If professional assistance is required, the services of a competent professional person should be sought.

Neither the publisher nor the author shall be liable for damages arising here-from. The fact that an organization or website is referred to in this work as a referred source of further information does not mean that the author or the publisher endorses the information the organization or Website may provide, or recommendations it may make. Further, readers should be aware that Internet Websites listed in this work may have changed or disappeared between when this work was written and when it was read. It is also advised that you review the potential financial and tax implications of any transaction with a qualified professional before proceeding.

Copyright © 2019 by Diego Rodriguez

DEDICATION

Dear Dad, I have thought long and hard about what I would say if I ever had the chance to speak to you again. My biggest regret is letting my ego get the best of me and not reaching out to you before you passed away. There are many memories, some good and some bad, that still remain in my heart. I am not trying to justify the wrong that was done, but the older I get the more I understand that in order to grow and continue moving forward in life we must learn to forgive to gain inner peace. Although you left my mother and I while I was still very young, I do want to thank you for leaving me with many valuable lessons and experiences that have served me throughout my life.

First, was the love and passion you passed on to me for Martial Arts. (Still have Bruce Lee poster on my wall!) I can still remember you teaching me how to do flips in the living room and placing the sofa cushions on the floor to break my falls. Martial Arts were and still are probably the most influential experience and practice in my life. Not only has it helped me defend myself growing up alone in the concrete jungle known as NYC, but it has also taught me disciple, focus and self respect! It has been the foundation that has given me the courage and sense of Honor to want a better life for our family! The next step for me was joining the Marine Corps, but it was those lesson learned about self awareness, discipline and courage that helped me overcome the temptations that existed while living in poverty, and trying to stay out of trouble long enough to earn my right to be called a US Marine and a man!

Second, was how you used to drag me every Saturday morning to work or some type of business meeting. While all the other kids spent their Saturday mornings enjoying their cartoons, I had to carry all the tools to help you fix leaky pipes in some tenant's apartment. If it wasn't that, then it was helping you carry your briefcase to some meeting in the middle of winter. That briefcase was almost as big as I was and probably weighed as much too…well, at least that's how it felt. I didn't know then (and boy did I hate you for it at the time) what I realize now that you were teaching me how to be a man and a warrior! Not only were you teaching me physically how to be 'handy' and self reliant, but also allowing me to observe how you became a self made, successful businessman. At a time when not many Dominican immigrants were known for owning their own businesses and real estate, you and mom still made it happen. You both were and still are my greatest mentors!

Rest in Peace Dad. Until we meet again…. I love you and will forever be thankful for all the lessons you taught me which continue serving me till this day! I would have never made it this far without your influence. –Your Warrior

INTRODUCTION

For those of you that don't know me, please allow me to introduce myself. My name is Diego Rodriguez. I am an author, real estate investor, entrepreneur, mentor, and creator of the 'BCB' Build Credit for your Business Workshop; helping entrepreneurs, business owners and start-ups establish and build over $100,000 in business credit to fuel their business goals and dreams, no longer held back due to lack of money! But by far, the title I am most proud of and honored to hold is being a United States Marine! "**Semper Fi!**" to all my Devil Dogs out there whether home or in harm's way. May God bless you all and bring you home to your families and loved ones safely.

Now for the rest of you, please don't feel left out. Welcome. I am honored that you have given me the opportunity to be a part of your entrepreneurial aspirations, and be a helping hand to get you on track. The purpose of this book is to serve as a guide in obtaining that pervasive dream of achieving FINANCIAL FREEDOM! And if you are reading this right now, then we probably have something in common. I did not come from a wealthy background. I had to hustle and break a sweat for every drop of money I earned...at first.

When you start out at $0 zero and living in poverty you don't have many choices. I always knew through the

examples my mother and father set at a very young age that hard work in a 9 to 5 job does pay the bills, but it doesn't free you from being a slave to that cycle of poverty. I saw how hard my mother was working and yes, she always provided for me, (God Bless her for that!), but I was not going to watch her just grow old and work herself to death.
And that is when my "WHY" was engraved into my heart. From that moment of realization, my goal became moving our family out of a crammed-up apartment and buying my mother a home! Through dedication and blessings, I was able to achieve my lifelong dream of buying her a home and now she works only 2 or 3 days just because it is her passion!

    I share this with you because becoming successful in business and in life does not happen by luck, and it doesn't come easy, or quickly. Life will put you to the test, over and over again to see what you are made of, and whether or not your dream or goal is genuine. The only true way of breaking out of the cycle of poverty and overcoming all the odds in my experience have been through:

1. <u>Education</u>- There are things in this world that we know we don't know, but oddly enough, there are even more things that we don't know we know! Not only must you expand your awareness, but also keep exercising that muscle in between your ears so it is fine-tuned when you need it the most!

2. <u>Owning Your Own Business</u>- You will have to work and work hard to become successful. So why not put all your time and energy in building your own 'job' and not someone else's.

3. <u>Defining Your "Why"</u>- the purpose or reason for doing what you do or what you aspire to become. This is by far the most important in my opinion of the 3 because you will get tested. You will fail many times before you get your first taste of success, however big or small. And if you don't have a "Why" deeply rooted within you, when life knocks you down, beating you with obstacle after obstacle, you will give up. Believe me… Life will put you to the test, if it's not already doing so as you are reading this.

So my advice to you is simple, if you have not discovered what you goals are yet, (besides of course seeking Financial Freedom), take a day or two to explore within you, what your purpose, your reason, your "WHY" for wanting Financial Freedom is! Once you have a clear and genuine picture of your answer, then it is all a matter of educating yourself and implementing what you have learned to reach your destination! And the path to Financial Freedom is through: **_GENERATING MULTIPLE STREAMS OF INCOME!_**

***All direct links for the Resources mentioned throughout this book are also provided in the 'Resource' Chapter at the end of this book for quicker reference!

*'Trust Your Gut,
Follow Your Heart,
Bet On Yourself,
...and Double Down!'
-Life*

Income Stream 1:

EARNED INCOME

L et's get one fact of life clear and out in the open… '**IT TAKES MONEY TO MAKE MONEY!**' No matter how you look at it or try to spin it, in order to create anything that will produce income it will take some sort of small investment in order to get it started. Whether it be educating yourself on 'how to', setting up shop to get the product or service created (overhead expenses: inventory, internet, etc…), or to promote and sell your product or service (advertising, marketing, etc..), you will need to make a small investment when starting out.

The #1 obstacle my students have in getting started on their journey to building wealth is not having money to begin with. So the million dollar question is "How am I supposed to make money if I don't have money?" Well, it doesn't mean it has to be your money! And No, that doesn't mean go ask your family or friends for money either. In my opinion, there is no greater feeling than knowing you have reached a level of success on your own two feet. What I am getting at here is the incredible leverage that Credit enables you to have, especially when you have no money of your own to begin with.

Having personal credit is great, but I am speaking about the vast and endless possibilities that establishing and building "Business Credit" can do for your business and life! If you wish to learn more, step-by-step instructions on how to establish a business from scratch on a shoestring budget; exactly where to apply; and how to build over $100k in business credit, then this course I created is made exactly with you in mind!

'BCB' Build Credit for your Business
(http://bit.ly/BusinessCredit100k)

Earned income is simply earning money by trading your time and labor for a paycheck. Or, you can get on the right path to becoming **Financially Free** by creating your own business and selling you own product or service! Most of you may not have your own product to sell at first. **The solution** = selling someone else's product and earning a decent commission every time you do. But the reality is that it will be difficult reaching the 6-7 figure paydays until you have created your own business product, service or both!

Income Stream 2:

Residual Income is the concept of getting paid, over and over again, well after you have put in the work, time and effort, by setting up a "System" in place to do the work for you! Unlike a regular job where you only get paid when you are physically at work (paid by the hour), the beauty of residual income is that you get paid around the clock, 24/7, regardless of where you are (in the office, at the beach, or in bed).

Learning and mastering the concept of having 'Systems" in place to conduct your daily business operations for you, for example...

- Getting leads/customers for your business,
- Following up with your leads,
- Online store/website,
- Marketing and advertising your products/services
- Sales presentations,
- Closing sales,
- Receiving payments (your automated cash register)

…will set you free to focus on other ways to produce income (or just enjoy life) and not have to sacrifice your time, becoming a slave to your own business. And again, most of you starting out do not have a product or service of your own to offer.

<u>The Solution</u> = [Team up with a Proven System and an income producing product]() that will do all the hard work for you and at the same time teach you how it is done… so you *can begin creating a business product or service of your own!* While you are getting an education on how to make money online, you will also get to use the same exact "**System**" we are using and make money together! You won't have to struggle on what products you need find or create to promote. You will also receive a Personal Coach to guide and help you through it all. All you have to do is go through the training, implement what we are teaching you and start collecting your $50, $300, $1,000 commissions!

If you are interested in learning more about this proven ["System"]() I am speaking about, then go to…

([http://bit.ly/SANPage]())

It is called the **Super Affiliate Network (SAN)**. In fact, we are so sure about this system that you can sign up for just $1… And if you are not actively making sales within 30 days, SAN will refund all your money and you would have still received the education for free! **A million dollar education for just a $1 investment**…

Income Stream 3:

ROYALTY INCOME

Now that we have addressed how to start making money today without having your own product to sell, let's get into the thrilling part of creating your own product. In my opinion, the best and shortest path to reaching a 7-figure income is by selling your own product or service! Sure you can make decent money selling other people's products, but what happens when that specific opportunity disappears... then what?

First of all, you should never depend on any one form of income, especially coming from someone else's hand! Secondly, by selling someone else's product, you are only getting a "commission", a fraction of the pot, when you could be earning your full share! That is why I highly advice you to start thinking about creating your own product.

By the way, if you have not read '**Think and Grow Rich**' by Napoleon Hill, you need to! Better yet... reach out to my Support Team at Support@univstrategies.com with the Subject "Diego said I should read 'Think and Grow Rich" and I will have them send you a copy for **free**. Right Mindset is Everything!

Now back on track... In my opinion, the quickest and simplest way to creating your own product is, **The Solution = Writing a Book!** A simple and informative topic, for example: how to cook healthy food, or how to wax your car, or how to paint and decorate your house, is all you need to get started. It doesn't have to be anything over the top. It should be though, something you are: Passionate about, Love doing (Hobby) and Can help/serve/inform others...

Don't worry about how long it should be, how you're going to sell it, or how 'rusty' you may be at writing. If you are passionate about the topic, then the book will write itself. You will be amazed on how it will come to life once you get your fingers hitting the keyboard! So grab your favorite cup of coffee, sit in your cozy spot and think about what you love doing the most. Whatever makes you feel alive and happy every time you are doing it... that is what you should write a book about! And don't worry about marketing and salesmanship. It is the *'invisible secret sauce'* that makes you successful, not the shinny object! If you are genuinely passionate about what you are marketing, selling, or creating, then my friend, that is what is going to sell and make you successful, not the shinny object itself!

When it comes to Royalty Income... have you ever heard of Amazon.com? (If you haven't, what planet are you from and do you come in peace?) Millions of people buy books, **daily**, from Amazon. And that is where and who will be doing the selling of your book for you! All you have to do is create the book and have Amazon publish it for you. So, because they will do all the work for you, every time a version of your book (Digital and Physical) is sold, you will receive a 'Royalty' check directly to your bank account, monthly! (Cha-Ching!!!)

If you need a [step-by-step educational course](#) on:

- How to set up your book to meet Amazon's requirements to submit for publishing.
- Interior and cover templates and layouts to use for writing your book.
- Graphics and tools to create your promotional materials to market your book (Because you don't want to just depend on Amazon to sell you book. You should be marketing it all over social media as well!)
- How-to videos to teach you everything you need to know about creating your book from scratch, promoting your book and selling your book!

[This amazing course](#) will even provide you with marketing tips, on "how to use keywords & categories on Amazon to maximize your book's reach," so you can get a better idea on what your book's topic should be to make it more attractive, marketable, and most importantly, **profitable**! It is the very exact course I took and stand by it 100%. When I started out, I had no clue on how it all works or how I was going to compete with all these "Best Selling" authors. But then I realized the most important piece of wisdom which I shared with you earlier in this chapter… **It is not the shiny object that sells, it is the Passion behind the object that attracts!**

The more passionate about the subject you are, the better and more attractive the subject will come across… hence, the better at selling it you will be **('The Invisible Secret Sauce'!)** Everything else is just putting the pieces of the puzzle together. This course teaches you and literally gives you all the pieces you need to put it together from step one: coming up with a concept, to final step: launching your book into the world! The name of the course… well it's more of a collection of courses and the name is:

"The Author Academy"
(http://bit.ly/AdazingAuthorAcademy)

If you wish to start creating your very own product and start collecting **Royalty Checks** then sign up! Perhaps the coolest part of creating your own book is that once it gets published; you have now created something that will outlast you, and remain part of this world forever! Just a tiny step on the path of creating your Legacy…

Income Stream 4:

INTEREST INCOME

Once you start generating your streams of income you will want **your money to work hard for you**! Some people are fine with keeping their money stored away safely, 'collecting dust' in a good old fashioned bank savings account. But what are the banks offering, maybe 1.5% interest, if you're lucky. Or perhaps, let them hold your money for a couple of years in a Certificate of Deposit and maybe get 3%. Banks are no fools! Sure they will safely store your money so you can earn a measly 1.5 to 3% in interest. And then, they turn around and charge you about 5% interest for a loan... **in best cases**, if you have perfect credit. So basically, they are charging you about 4x as much, minimum, when only paying you 1.5% interest in a savings account to use your money!

What we need to do is adapt their mindset, by becoming "Banks" ourselves through lending money. Yes, there is always a risk of not being paid back, but when done right, with the right people and the right "**System**", you can minimize the risks and capitalize on the rewards! So instead of receiving only 1-3% interest in return for lending your money to a bank (via Savings account, CD's, etc.), why not lend money yourself and collect 8-12+% interest on your hard earned money?

For those of you familiar with Real Estate Investing, you may already know the concept of private lending or 'Hard Money Loans', were private individuals (or companies) lend money for short terms. They are much more lenient on loan requirements, but do demand a higher interest rate in return because of it! Now, most of you may not have a stock pile of cash sitting somewhere to lend $50-100k+ to investors and collect 8-12% checks monthly in interest. But, there is a "**System**" available for you to become a lender by making smaller loans and start collecting monthly payments in Interest Income! The name of the company is called:

"The Lending Club"
(http://bit.ly/LendingClubVest)

Lending Club acts as the middleman between, people applying for loans (ranging anywhere up to $40,000), and 'Investors' seeking to lend their money. Lending Club has a **'System'** in place where you can lend as little as $25 per requested loan. And the best part is that you, as the 'Investor', do not have to lend the entire loan amount requested. Let's say for example the loan requested is $5,000. Lending Club pools together all the money it's 'Investors' are lending to fund the total ($5,000 in this example). So you as the 'Investor' get to decide how much of your money you want to lend on any one specific note/loan. You can lend as little as $25... Yes that's right, as little as $25 in each individual loan requested. But, there is a $1,000 initial minimum to open your Lending Club account to begin lending as an 'Individual'. If you wish to open an account as a 'Corporation' then the minimum is much higher depending on your business history.

Lending Club does all the work in screening the 'Applicants' as far as credit history, public records, delinquencies, etc. And the higher the risk is, the higher the interest the 'Investor' is rewarded. You can easily receive monthly interest payments from your notes/loans averaging 10-12%, depending on your risk tolerance. If you prefer safer loans then you can average 6-8%, still beating your bank's saving accounts of only 1.5-3% interest.

The smart strategy, to minimize your risk while still receiving decent interest (7-12% returns) would be to spread your money over several notes/loans, not just one. You can lend as little as $25 per each note. So if you spread, or divide your initial $1,000 into $25 notes, you can easily invest in 40 different notes. (40 notes x $25 invest in each = $1,000). Now you are collecting monthly interest on 40 different notes, ranging in different interest rates, depending on the risk level you feel comfortable with. Let's go conservative and say you are only willing lend on safer notes paying out an average of 7%. If we do the Math, 40 notes x $25 each invested = $1,000 x 7% interest comes out to about $70 in annual interest. And if we divide that **monthly** ($70/12 months) you are making about $5.83 in interest. This may seem like a small amount, but how much are you making now in a bank account paying you only 1.5% interest, if you only had $1,000…. about $1.25/month at most?

Adding on to this strategy, continue reinvesting your interest into more notes and **compounding your interest** (Picture a small snowball rolling down hill, getting bigger and bigger and at same time, picking up speed!). In this scenario we're only investing the initial requirement of $1,000. Using our example of conservative 7%, your monthly interest income is about $5.83, and if you reinvest it (by waiting until it adds up to another $25), then you can invest in another note, and now have 41 total notes receiving interest. Now your monthly interest income goes up to $5.93, and continuing to compound! And remember these are only conservative figures at 7%. What if you purchased notes paying 10% interest? Your income, with same initial investment of $1,000, now becomes about $8.33 in monthly interest.

And what if monthly you add small increments of money on top of your initial $1,000 investment? Once you open your account you can continue to add more money, and you can transfer much lower amounts now that you have an active account. Can you see where this is going? The compound interest affect is awesome when done correctly!

Please keep in mind: If all you had to your name was $1,000, then this strategy would **not** be for you… This is based on you already making some money, and putting **some** of your saved money to work much harder for you at a much higher return, instead of just 'collecting dust' in a bank's savings account!

*'If You Do
What You've Always Done,
You'll Get
What You've Always Gotten'
-Tony Robbins*

Income Stream 5:

DIVIDEND INCOME

For my stock market aficionados out there, this one you will enjoy. And if you are not familiar with investing in stocks, then let me be the first to welcome you to yet another stream of income! If you are already dabbling in buying stocks then you are aware that some stocks offer dividends (the act of companies rewarding their investors by distributing a small percentage of their annual profits; usually paid out quarterly), while other stocks do not. Our focus here is on stocks that do pay out dividends to their loyal shareholders!

Depending on which brokerage firm you already use or choose to start investing in stocks with, (I like TDAmeritrade… only $6.95/trade) you will have a wide range of companies to choose from that are paying dividends. Our focus here is on companies that have a proven history of paying out dividends (Dividend Yield). Specifically, stocks with at least a 7 years+ history of not just paying out dividends, but also steadily growing the amount they are paying out (Dividend Growth). Luckily, to facilitate this research, there already exists such a list. So you don't have to go crazy searching high and low for these hidden gems. Get it here: (http://Dripinvesting.org)

The list of companies that have a proven history of paying out dividends is called "**U.S. Dividend Champions**" (25 years+). Then there are the other companies with fewer amounts of years of proven dividend payout called "**Contenders**" (10-24yrs) and "**Challengers**" (5-9yrs). I like to stick with companies that have a minimum of 7 years of proven dividend payout.

Now, as far as how much money you will need to invest in order to start applying this strategy depends on:

1) What the minimum investment would be for you to open a brokerage account and start implementing this strategy, if you don't already have a brokerage account to begin with,
2) What the price of the individual dividend paying stock(s) of your choice is at the time of purchase.
3) This will also determine how many different dividend paying stocks you can start adding to your portfolio, using this strategy.

If you are starting with a small investment (Less than $10k) this strategy is more beneficial on a long-term basis to build up your retirement nest egg, and can then be used as a decent monthly income, once you do retire. You can still use this strategy to start earning income now, but again, as described in the previous chapter, especially when starting small, it's about compounding your interest (Allowing the snowball to keep growing and picking up steam the longer you let it roll down hill). And the younger you start, ages 21-30's versus ages 40-50's, is a difference in $Millions once you are ready for retirement. **This strategy alone can make you a millionaire upon retirement!** Below is a table to show a ruff example of how the longer you keep a stock, the more momentum and effective compounding interest can be. Keep in mind, we are reinvesting the dividends back into buying more shares and assuming you are not investing any more money.

Example of initial investment $10k and reinvesting the dividends				
Initial Div Yield	Div Growth Rate	Value after: 5yrs	10yrs	20yrs
4%	8%	$13,199	$19,062	$60,732
4%	10%	$13,320	$20,104	$89,294
5%	8%	$13,967	$21,821	$90,200

Can you see the incredible affect compound interest has from year 10 to year 20 by just simply reinvesting the dividends? You can double your money in nearly 10 years and 6x as much after 20yrs by only reinvesting your dividends. Now imagine if you steadily kept investing more money throughout the first 5 to 10 year span!!! It doesn't matter how much money you start out with, the incredible affects still apply to any amount. This table is from the book I highly recommend you read to get further detail on how to research these dividend paying stocks.

Copyright © 2019 by Diego Rodriguez

And the creator of this strategy is Marc Lichtenfeld, author of the awesome book "Get Rich with Dividends"! *Did I mention I highly recommend you read it to dig deeper into this stream of income?* I am only briefly touching upon the benefits behind it and how the formula works. I will be adding a video to my blog (www.Univstrategies.com/blog) to get into it more in detail on how I research the companies I choose to add to my own Dividend Income Portfolio. **So keep on the lookout for my email notifications**! I would like us to build our own little investment community where we can compare our selections and help each other build our own 'Dividend Income Portfolios', creating a community of millionaires!!! Go to the link below to get your copy…

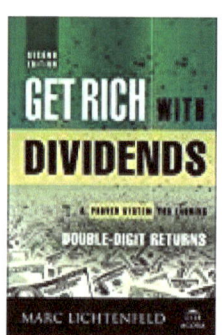

**"Get Rich with Dividends:
A Proven System for Earning Double-Digit Returns"
(http://bit.ly/GetRichDividends)**

In the book, Marc writes about a simple formula: **'The 10-11-12 System'** to apply this strategy. The '10' represents the number of years you want to keep this strategy compounding for you, but as you can see from our table, this really gets juicy at the 15-20 year mark. But let's stick the formula. The '11' represents the average percent, over 10 years, which your dividend yield (dividend payout) would have grown to. And the '12' represent the total annual return from your stock, after 10yrs. This includes the Dividend Yield % plus the Capital Gains %. Capital Gains are simply the rise, or drop in price of the stock versus what you originally paid for it.

So for my mathematicians, if you noticed, more weight is put on the percentage of growth on the dividend yield (payout) than whether or not the stock price rises or falls after 10 years from original purchase. In fact, as prices fall, the more shares of stocks you can buy as you reinvest your dividends. (Another <u>Benefit</u> of the Compound Interest Strategy!!!)

I don't want to get into too much detail here, but in order to achieve 11% dividend yield and 12% average annual returns in 10 years, you will need to take into account some key requirements when purchasing a stock today. There are a few mentioned in the book, but basically:

- It should be a stock with proven history of paying out dividends,
- Proven history of growing the dividends paid out of about a 10% Dividend Growth,
- And the current Dividend Yield should be at about 4.7% or higher.

There are a few other factors to screen your choices of stocks with also, so please <u>read the book</u>!!!

When it comes to investing, you know the age old theory "never put all your eggs in one basket". But if you can only afford to buy one stock starting out, then you should not spread yourself too thin either! If I had less than $2,500 to invest, then I would start with one stock and made sure it hit all our requirements in the 10-11-12 formula. If I had $5k then I would pick 3 different stocks, **each in a different market sector**. Don't just try to tap into whatever market is hot today. Remember, we just came out of the housing crisis. How many of you would have dared to invest in a Real Estate stock? Not many, well… maybe Warren Buffet! ;-)

In the book, Marc mentions his own portfolio which he has created implementing the 10-11-12 formula. He does not state specifically which stocks he chose, but he does briefly list which market sectors he's invested in. After all, the greatest teachers teach you how to fish, NOT catch the fish for you, right? (The true lesson is learning how to feed yourself and not having to be fed. Never depend on someone else's hand to eat!) In his portfolio, he chose about 18 different markets/sectors to invest in. I have no idea how much money or what percentage in each individual sector he chose to invest.

I chose to create my own portfolio but with only 12 different stocks, each in a different market sector, and still following the same '**10-11-12 System**', for my dividend paying machine! Most of you starting out may not have the money to spread throughout 12 different market sectors, so just start with 1-3 stocks and then let is slowly build into more stocks! The point is to start now so you can reap the reward much later in life when trying to hustle and build will be much more difficult on you physically, mentally and economically!

And just because I am doing something a certain way, does not mean you can't figure out a better or smarter way of doing it. You should always do what feels right, and identifies with who you are and what your situation at this time may be. We all have teachers, but you do not gain wisdom until you can make those lessons your own!

>>> **Read the Book 'Get Rich with Dividends'!!!**

'The Universe Has No Restrictions. You Place Restrictions On The Universe With Your Expectations.'
-Deepak Chopra

Income Stream 6:

PROFIT INCOME

This one is a pretty much common sense, right? *Profit* – the act of selling something for more than what you paid for it! In the previous chapter, we spoke about 'Dividend Income' being an additional benefit when it comes to investing in stocks. But let's not forget the fundamental benefit, being able to buy stocks at a lower price and selling them for a profit, at a higher price. Now, becoming a savvy stock investor... well, that would take an entirely separate book! And if you enjoy sitting in front of your computer, and ripping your hair out every time your stock dips in price, then this is perfect for you! (Joking... but not really ;-) But if you would like to learn more, and get tips from experts on how and which stocks to buy to turn profits quickly then go here and sign up for:

"THE OXFORD CLUB NEWSLETTER"
(oxfordclub.com)

There is a recurring debate on how the wealthiest people of the world became rich. It is said that the majority of the richest people in the world became so by investing in Real Estate. Now, I'm not refuting this statement, but I do believe it is a bit misleading. After all, it's how I got started making real money, profiting more money in each deal than what most people earn in a year! But most people do not start making their money through investing in Real Estate. The majority of the richest people in the world first got started making money by creating their own companies, inventing their own unique products or services. And then, once their businesses took off and became profitable, they needed another avenue to 'Grow' their money! Real Estate provided that shelter. Once they started investing their profits into Real Estate, then the real building of wealth manifested and became solidified!

There are 3 things all humans need to survive: Food, Water, and **Shelter**. There will always be a demand for homes, especially with a growing population! Wealthy people know how to profit from these necessities and at the same time, **make their money work for them**! This is key in continuing to build wealth, instead of hoarding money under lock and key, in a bank savings account, collecting dust. Real Estate is not only one of the best avenues to amass wealth, but it also gives you the ability to conserve your earnings by deducting your income tax liabilities.

Most of the Tax Laws in this country (USA) are made to reward the business and land owners. I won't go into how many tax write-offs are available for you by owning real estate because first, I am not a tax attorney, nor a CPA. Second, it's way too boring! But I will say this: When it comes to buying and selling real estate, you can make good money in the short term (less than 1 year), but you will get hit hard by taxes (Short Term Gains). The real benefits of investing in real estate are long term holds to really reap the rewards of owning property, which we will get into in the next chapters. If you can hold a real estate investment for more than 1 year, then you are only getting hit by 'Long Term Capital Gains' tax, which is much lower than the 'Short Term Gains' tax, if you choose to sell the property! Also, if you are analyzing your property's value correctly at time of purchase, and the conditions of the market place are favorable, waiting 1 year+ should turn even greater profits due to rise in value.

"Buy low, Sell High", sound familiar? Real Estate has always been a market than runs in cycles. (Picture a rollercoaster ride). Depending on where your market is currently, it may be riding high at the moment, but after a few years, it starts to plateau and eventually drops back down. After a few years of 'recovery' at the bottom, it inevitably begins to rise again, following the same cycle, over and over again. So always buy when market is low, and <u>sell on the rise</u>!

Knowing where in the cycle your current real estate market is will set you apart from the average investor. To learn more about real estate market cycles read this book by David Lindahl:

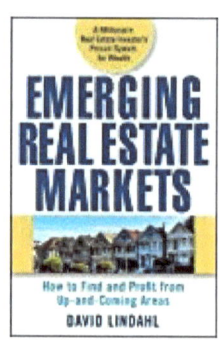

"Emerging Real Estate Markets: How to Find and Profit from Up-and-Coming Areas"
(http://bit.ly/EmergingREMarkets)

As mentioned earlier, I got my start in Real Estate. And Yes, I '*lost*' a ton of money trying to learn. I put the word lost in quotes because looking back… it was more of an investment into my education, although it didn't feel like it at the time! Many a book, course and mentorship did I suffer through, spending my life savings in trying to become a real estate investor. And while most gurus were teaching the same basic theories, their main focus was on keeping you needing more help, so you would have to keep paying into a more expensive package or training.

That being said, if I didn't go through all that '*Education*', I probably would have never crossed paths with my one true Real Estate Mentor, Lex Levinrad. After being over $50k in the whole, losing all of my life saving, but still left with a burning desire to become successful, I guess God said "Ok, now you are ready!" Who was it that said, "The Teacher only appears when the Student is ready"? I had no money left, but I still found a way to make it happen, and the power of Business Credit was my salvation (Besides God of course, and the right Mentor!)

I learned not only how to buy a property, fix it up, and then sell it; but you can also be the middleman and still make money! The strategy is called '**Wholesaling**', where you basically find a property, get it under contract and sell it to the next person, for a small profit, while still leaving enough 'meat on the bone' for the next person to make money on the deal. This was perfect for me getting started since I had no money for holding onto a property. Then, as I started cashing small checks (averaging $10k each), and Building my Business Credit along side, I was able to really get into the real estate investment game by holding onto properties! If you would like to learn more from my very own mentor in Real Estate, the awesome Mr. Lex Levinrad himself, then: **LEARN REAL ESTATE FROM THE BEST**... and tell him I sent you!

Get your free copy of his bestselling book on how to 'Wholesale' real estate properties…
(http://bit.ly/REWholesaleBook)

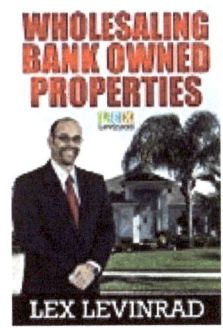

Copyright © 2019 by Diego Rodriguez

Or you can go to the link below to **get a free webinar class** on how Lex's students are flipping houses without using any of their own cash, implementing the strategies I mentioned earlier, and you can too! I am living proof this is for real! You can partner with him if you don't have any money of your own to flip houses!!! Go to the link below for his free webinar class:

"HOW LEX'S STUDENTS ARE FLIPPING HOUSES WITHOUT USING ANY OF THEIR OWN CASH!"
(http://bit.ly/FlippingHousesWeb)

Income Stream 7:

RENTAL INCOME

You build your empire one property at a time, is what I would tell my younger self if I could travel back in time! Two of the most common types of real estate properties to invest in are Commercial and Residential Real Estate. My preference is in Residential Real Estate. Like I stated previously, people will always need a place to live in order to survive. The same can't be said about Commercial Real Estate, which focuses on business spaces. Businesses come and go, especially now with most commerce being sold online and entrepreneurs making money right from their own homes.

Investing in Rental Property is not a cake walk, and although I may make it seem so, I am only giving you a brief overview. There are many lessons to learn before becoming a 'Real Estate Rental Mogul'. My purpose here is to make you aware of this important stream of income if your goal is to hit beyond 7 figures in income streams and build your empire!

Investing in rental properties comes with its own set of headaches. There will always be a need to maintain your properties; fix a leaky pipe, unclog a toilet and of course, when dealing with tenants, always the risk of them not paying rent. But that is why you should get in the habit of building **'Systems'** for yourself! Have someone else do all the dirty work for you. All you need to be concerned about is receiving your 'Rental Income' check every month directly into your bank account!

The '**System**' I am referring to, in this case, is hiring a Property Manager! You should never be the one receiving phone calls at 3am from a tenant because the toilet is clogged up! Finding the right Property Manager for your properties is vital if you want to maintain your sanity and valuable time that should be spent looking for the next investment! Sure the Property Manager with charge you about 8-10% of the rents collected. But trust me, finding the right one to take care of all the day-to-day operations is well worth ever cent! Go visit your local **Real Estate Investment Clubs**. They are an excellent source of information to find out who the good property managers are, as well as investor friendly lenders and deals for your next rental property!

Depending on how much of your own money you can afford to purchase a property with versus how much of a loan you would have to take out to cover the rest, will be the biggest factor in whether or not your rental properties will generate positive cash flow. The other factors, but not limited to, will be: location, property taxes, insurance, property management, and maintenance expenses. As you can gather, the expenses add up quickly. So you may not make a huge amount of Rental Income, or positive cash flow, on your first property. It may be just a couple of hundred dollars, depending on how much of a mortgage loan you had to borrow. But focus on the big picture… the beauty is that when done right, your monthly rents will not only pay for the property itself, including all expenses, but it will also leave you will with some extra cash.

A good rule of thumb to have when deciding how much to pay for purchase of a rental property is using the **'1% Rule'**. For example, let's say after researching (www.rentometer.com) how much the average rent being paid in the neighborhood of your choice for a 3 bedroom home is about $1,200/month. Using our 1% Rule, you should only be paying about $120,000 to purchase that property. Now, depending on where in the real estate cycle your market may be in, (as we discussed in the previous chapter), it may be impossible to buy a 3 bedroom home at this price. If so, then either the market prices are already riding too high and it is not the right time to buy-and-hold or you are not searching in the ideal neighborhood. You should be buying rental properties in middle class family neighborhoods; not the high class, and not the 'war zone' areas. It is the middle class families with decent jobs that will be your bread and butter of reliable tenants!

The 1% Rule is just a quick calculation for you to get a better sense of a decent purchase price for a rental property.

If you can afford to make a greater down payment, or not need a mortgage loan to acquire the property, then more power to you. But in my opinion, you should not be putting down so much of your own money into just 1 rental property alone. You can use that same amount of money perhaps as a down payment to purchase 2 rental properties, and mortgage the rest. Never get greedy though… If the numbers don't work then walk away and continue looking, or wait until the ideal time of the market cycle presents itself!

Keep in mind that the more bedrooms your property has the more rent you can charge! The ideal rental property should have at least 3 bedrooms, and a garage, with no pool. Pools and tenants don't mix!!! It's a huge liability if God forbid, someone drowns or gets hurt! Finding a home with 4 bedrooms as a rental would be great, but difficult to find at a decent price. Ideally, a 3 bedrooms home with 2 bathrooms, a garage and no pool, is what I look for in a rental. Focus on who your target market of tenants are. Where would they want to live, raise their children and have to pay rent?

As you begin to generate more and more income from your 'Multiple Streams of Income' you can then afford to buy the next property with a bigger down payment, and require less of a mortgage loan. This will produce even more positive cash flow from rental income, at the end of the month. And then you can buy the next one, and then the next… Can you see where this is headed?!

Build Your Empire One Property At A Time!

Income Stream 8:

We have already discussed the basic strategies investing in stocks. You can profit from stocks by buying at a low price and then selling them at a higher price. Also, and my favorite, is buying dividend paying stocks because you can buy them and not have to sell them in order to make money. The dividends paid out from these stocks can generate a steady stream of income for you to use for another investment, or simply reinvest them back into buying more dividend paying stocks.

Not only are you collecting yet another stream of income, but also benefiting from the natural progression of a growing stock market. That is where 'Capital Gains' come in. Yes, there have been years of market drops, but in the long run, the overall average value of the stock market has been steadily climbing. I love dividend paying stocks because of the short and long term benefits. Not only are they paying me a steady amount of dividend (short term= every quarter), but I can hold on to the stock for the **long term** and ride the overall rise of the stock market, increasing the overall value of my stock portfolio! Because you are receiving dividends in the short term, there is no need to sell the stock. Hold on to them and keep adding to your dividend stock portfolios. Before you know it, the dividend income alone will be enough to cover your monthly expenses. This strategy will also reward you with steady income during retirement, and all the while the overall value of your portfolio is also increasing (Capital Gains)!

Investing in real estate rental properties is another one of my loves and very similar to the strategy behind dividend paying stocks. Now, instead of collecting dividends from stocks, I am collecting rents from tenants! And when the strategy is applied right, as the years pass, the tenant is paying all the expenses of property for me, as I continue to raise the rents year after year. Similar to the stock market, the real estate market has its own cycles. If you buy at the right time when the market is at a low point and hold onto the property, you will not only benefit from the rental income, but the rise in property value as well (Capital Gain)!

As you can see, investors in it for the long haul tend to be the ones that come out on top by building wealth. Those that jump in to make a quick buck can surely get lucky, but we don't want to establish wealth based on luck now, do we? Learn from the ones that have been successful, and then sculpt each strategy to fit your goals. When it comes to building wealth, always plan for the long term!

CONCLUSION

Once you free yourself from the burdens of having to live paycheck to paycheck, you will soon realize that making money and generating streams of income becomes a game! With continued education and implementing the right strategies, it just becomes a matter of moving pieces on a chessboard to reach your desired outcome! There will always be obstacles in Life to overcome, but once you free yourself from the burden of needing money just to survive, and learn how to play the game, Life's obstacles become that much smoother to deal with and overcome. The secret to playing the money game is generating multiple streams of income! Now the secret to the Game of Life… well, that's a whole other ballgame! ;-)

I look forward to hearing your stories of success and **reviews of this book on Amazon!** Any questions or concerns you may have, you can always reach out to our team at: Support@univstrategies.com. I have briefly touched upon each individual stream of income, but for a more in-depth education use the resources I have shared with you throughout each chapter and listed at the end of this book titled **'Resources'**. Depending on what version of this book you are reading, they should all be hyperlinked for you to access easier and quicker.

Keep a look out for my email notifications, as I will be sharing educational videos to cover more details on current and future Streams of Income! If you are not currently on our mailing list, please make sure you visit our website at: www.univstrategies.com and sign up to our mailing list.

Hopefully, you will implement some, if not all the strategies mentioned in this book to start not only making money, but freeing yourself and living Life the way it was meant to be. **Master the art of making your money work hard for you or you will have to work hard for it!** Your first step is to decide to make a change. Your second step is to take action! The true path to becoming wealthy is by creating your own business, selling your own product or service. If you don't have your own product at first, then start your own business by selling someone else's product or service, as mentioned in the second chapter **'Residual Income'**, in a proven system that will not only educate you, but will also pay you as you are learning by earning $50, $300, & $1,000 commission checks!

As you are learning and making money, think about what you can create as your own product or service. That my friend is your ticket to 7 figures! Go back to chapter one **'Earned Income'** and let's establish and build your own business. And if you have no clue as to what product you can create or service you should provide, I will leave you with this one quote:

*"Where Your Talents and the Needs of the World Cross, There Lies Your Vocation." -**Aristotle***

Copyright © 2019 by Diego Rodriguez

RESOURCES

Stream One: Earned Income Resource(s):
Learn how to Establish a Business, Build over $100k in Business Credit & Exactly where to Apply!
- http://bit.ly/BusinessCredit100k

Stream Two: Residual Income Resource(s):
If you do not have a product of your own to sell then join our team and start making real money from home, even if you're Brand New and on a Shoestring Budget!
- http://bit.ly/SANPage

Stream Three: Royalty Income Resource(s):
Create your very own product and have Amazon sell it for you!
- http://bit.ly/AdazingAuthorAcademy

Stream Four: Interest Income Resource(s):
Earn money like the banks do. Become a lender and receive 8-12% interest.
- http://bit.ly/LendingClubVest

Stream Five: Dividend Income Resource(s):
Learn a Proven System for earning double-digit returns investing in Dividend paying stocks.
- Dividend Strategy Book: http://bit.ly/GetRichDividends

To learn more visit us at: www.univstrategies.com

Copyright © 2019 by Diego Rodriguez

Stream Six: Profit Income Resource(s):
Learn how to Wholesale and Flip Houses directly from the man who taught me!
- Free Wholesaling Book:
    http://bit.ly/REWholesaleBook
- Free Real Estate Webinar Class:
    http://bit.ly/FlippingHousesWeb
- Emerging Real Estate Markets Book:
    http://bit.ly/EmergingREMarkets

Stream Seven: Rental Income Resource(s):
- Become a Real Estate Mogul- Free Webinar
    http://bit.ly/REFlipMogul

Additional Resources for building your money making, wealth building Empire!
- Open up your own online store like the professionals do and try it out for **FREE** for 14 days:
    http://bit.ly/ClickFunnelsPro

Copyright © 2019 by Diego Rodriguez

www.ingramcontent.com/pod-product-compliance
Lightning Source LLC
Chambersburg PA
CBHW040246220526
45473CB00001B/384